Dinosaur Stalkers in the Swamp

by Paul Mason

Illustrated by
Andre Leonard

HUNGRY TOMATO™

MINNEAPOLIS

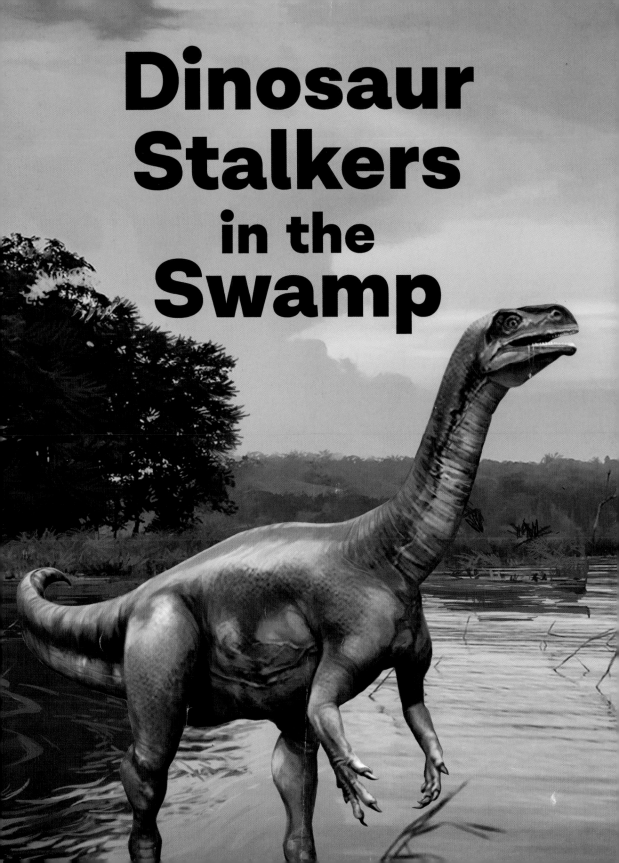

Dinosaur Stalkers in the Swamp

Thanks to the creative team:
Senior Editor: Alice Peebles
Consultant: Neil Clark
Design: Perfect Bound Ltd

Original edition copyright 2018 by Hungry Tomato Ltd.
Copyright © 2019 by Lerner Publishing Group, Inc.

Hungry Tomato® is a trademark of Lerner Publishing Group

Hungry Tomato®
A division of Lerner Publishing Group, Inc.
241 First Avenue North
Minneapolis, MN 55401 USA

For reading levels and more information, look up
this title at www.lernerbooks.com.

Main body text set in Graviola Soft 12/14.

Library of Congress Cataloging-in-Publication Data

Names: Mason, Paul, 1967– author. | Leonard, Andre, 1954– illustrator.
Title: Dinosaur stalkers in the swamp / Paul Mason, Andre Leonard.
Description: Minneapolis : Hungry Tomato, [2018] | Series: Dinosaurs rule | Audience: Ages 8-12. |
Audience: Grades 4 to 6.
Identifiers: LCCN 2018002093 (print) | LCCN 2018010802 (ebook) | ISBN 9781541523982 (eb pdf)
| ISBN 9781541501027 (lb : alk. paper)
Subjects: LCSH: Dinosaurs—Juvenile literature. | Dinosaurs—Behavior—Juvenile literature.
Classification: LCC QE861.5 (ebook) | LCC QE861.5 .M34298 2018 (print) | DDC 567.9—dc23

LC record available at https://lccn.loc.gov/2018002093

Manufactured in the United States of America
1-43773-33631-4/19/2018

Contents

World of the Dinosaurs

Dinosaurs lived on Earth during the Triassic, Jurassic, and Cretaceous Periods. At first they competed with other animals. During the Jurassic Period, though, dinosaurs began to dominate the world.

Dinosaurs spread across almost every part of the world. Many lived in or near swamps—places where there was soft ground, water, and lots of plants.

Triassic world
(250–201 million years ago)

At this time, the main land on Earth was a "supercontinent" called Pangea. Pangea had a dry interior, with few rivers or lakes, so swamps were found mainly in coastal areas.

Jurassic world
(201–145 million years ago)

During the Jurassic Period, Pangea broke up and formed new, more mountainous lands. Rivers began to flow from the newly formed mountains to the seas, so swamps became more common.

Cretaceous world
(145–66 million years ago)

During this last age of the dinosaurs, Earth's lands changed again and today's continents began to form. Rivers, lakes, and swamps all became more common. For hungry predators, the swamps were an excellent hunting ground.

Clash of the Giants!
Tyrannosaurus vs. *Triceratops*

This is a battle between giants. *Tyrannosaurus* is hoping to bring down a massive meal—but its prey won't be easy to kill.

Triceratops has a neck frill for protection, and the long, pointed horns on its forehead could inflict a deadly wound.

Tyrannosaurus

Tyrannosaurus was one of the biggest carnivorous dinosaurs ever. It was probably too heavy to run very fast, but its main prey was big, slow-moving dinosaurs such as *Edmontosaurus* and *Triceratops*.

Once *Tyrannosaurus* caught victims, they were in trouble. *Tyrannosaurus*'s mouth was lined with over 50 blade-like teeth that bit down with tremendous force. And like other dinosaurs, if *Tyrannosaurus*'s teeth wore out or were damaged, new ones grew to replace them.

KILLER FACT

Experts think *Tyrannosaurus* might have been able to rip off more than 440 lb (200 kg) of flesh in a single bite.

SCALE

Top speed
In 2017, scientists suggested that *Tyrannosaurus* could run as fast as 18 mph (29 km/h), about the same as a running human.

FACT FILE

Alive: 68–65 million years ago
Order and Family: Saurischia/ Tyrannosauridae
Length: 39 ft. (12 m)
Height: 11 ft. 9 in. (3.6 m)
Weight: 6.6 tons (6 t)
Diet: carnivorous
Fossils found: skulls and skeletons, so every part of this dinosaur is known
Location: west-central and north-central United States

KILLER FACT

Fossilized *Triceratops* frills show that their surface was covered in blood vessels. *Triceratops* may have been able to flush its frill with blood, creating a colorful display.

Triceratops was probably the most common big plant eater in North America—making young *Triceratops* a common target for *Tyrannosaurus*.

However, *Triceratops* was not defenseless: its horns would have been dangerous to predators. One fossilized horn has been found with a partly-healed *Tyrannosaurus* bite. Because the bite began to heal, we know that the *Triceratops* survived the attack.

Scaly?

Pieces of *Triceratops* skin have been found that seem to be covered in large scales, some with cone-shaped bumps. They may have been for protection.

FACT FILE

Alive: 68–65 million years ago
Order and Family: Ornithischia/ Ceratopsidae
Length: 26 ft. (8 m)
Height: 9 ft. 10 in. (3 m)
Weight: 9.9 tons (9 t)
Diet: herbivorous
Fossils found: skulls and skeletons, so every part of this dinosaur is known
Location: north-central United States; south-central Canada

SCALE

Chase through the Swamp
Neovenator vs. Mantellisaurus

Neovenator is chasing after what looks like an easy meal. If it can just catch one of these young *Mantellisaurus*, it can use its size and fearsome jaws to kill it.

Neovenator's size is causing it problems, though. The big predator is getting bogged down in the swamp—unlike the *Mantellisaurus*.

Neovenator

Neovenator was an apex predator—a hunter that nothing else hunted. It was well armed with a mouth full of sharp, serrated teeth and strong arms tipped with long claws.

Although Neovenator was long and tall, it had slim bones. This suggests that it was relatively light and quite speedy. It would have been able to chase down prey such as a *Mantellisaurus*, or perhaps a young *Polacanthus*.

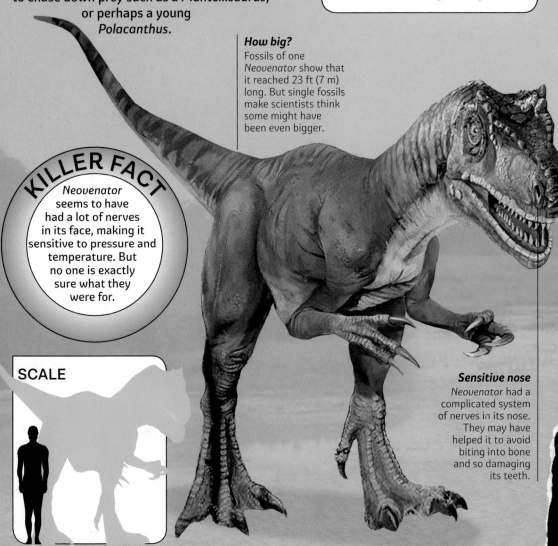

How big?
Fossils of one Neovenator show that it reached 23 ft (7 m) long. But single fossils make scientists think some might have been even bigger.

KILLER FACT

Neovenator seems to have had a lot of nerves in its face, making it sensitive to pressure and temperature. But no one is exactly sure what they were for.

SCALE

Sensitive nose
Neovenator had a complicated system of nerves in its nose. They may have helped it to avoid biting into bone and so damaging its teeth.

Mantellisaurus

Mantellisaurus was the same length as *Neovenator*, but not nearly as heavy. When feeding on low-level plants, it probably stood on all four legs. Because its front legs were shorter, its mouth would then have been at feeding level.

If *Mantellisaurus* had to run away, though, it probably used only two legs. Its longer, more powerful back legs would have been faster than scurrying on all fours.

SCALE

Grinding teeth
As an herbivore, *Mantellisaurus* had flat teeth on both sides of its jaw for grinding up tough plants.

Stiff tail
Like many dinosaurs, *Mantellisaurus* had a stiff tail, which it held out straight behind to balance its body weight.

FACT FILE

Alive: 125–110 million years ago
Order: Ornithischia
Length: 23 ft. (7 m)
Height: 7 ft. 2 in. (2.2 m)
Weight: adult size uncertain, probably about 1,650 lb. (750 kg)
Diet: herbivorous
Fossils found: an almost-complete skull and most of the skeleton
Location: Isle of Wight, southeast England

Sneaky Raider
Liliensternus vs. *Plateosaurus*

A snack like this won't fill up *Liliensternus*—but it has spotted something bigger.

If *Liliensternus* can launch a fast attack, it might be able to separate the baby *Plateosaurus* from the older one. That baby dinosaur would make a *big* meal.

Liliensternus

As the largest meat eater at this time, *Liliensternus* would have been an apex predator. It was far lighter than later predators of similar length—*Albertosaurus*, for example, was only half as long again as *Liliensternus* but weighed almost 20 times as much!

Its light weight meant that *Liliensternus* was able to run fast on two legs. As it leaned forward to chase prey, its tail stuck out stiffly behind for balance.

FACT FILE

Alive: 228–208 million years ago
Order: Saurischia
Length: 17 ft. (5.2 m)
Height: 4 ft. 3 in. (1.3 m)
Weight: 287 lb. (130 kg)
Diet: carnivorous
Fossils found: a skull and many parts of the skeleton
Location: Switzerland; central Germany

SCALE

Speedy hunter
Liliensternus was fast enough to catch small, quick dinosaurs and reptiles and maybe even flying creatures too.

Careful stalker
Liliensternus may have crept up as close as possible on large prey before attacking. Against this prey, its big, slashing teeth were the main weapon.

Plateosaurus

Plateosaurus's main defense was its size. Even *Liliensternus*—the biggest predator around— was far smaller. But *Plateosaurus*'s size could be a problem in the swamps of the late Triassic Period. If it wandered onto soft, muddy ground in search of food (or was chased there), a fully grown *Plateosaurus* could sink in. Struggling to get free, it sank further into the mud, became trapped, and died.

FACT FILE

Alive: 214–204 million years ago
Order and Family: Saurischia/ Plateosauridae
Length: 27 ft. 10 in. (8.5 m)
Height: 9 ft. 10 in. (3 m)
Weight: 2 tons (1.9 t)
Diet: herbivorous
Fossils found: skulls and skeletons, so this dinosaur is well known
Location: southern Germany

Long neck
Plateosaurus had a small head (and tiny brain) at the end of a long, flexible neck that helped it reach inaccessible plants.

SCALE

On two legs
This dinosaur walked on two legs. Its arms had three long claws, useful for defense and when feeding.

19

Attack from the Water

Deinosuchus vs. *Appalachiosaurus*

All this young *Appalachiosaurus* really wanted was a drink—instead, it got a nasty surprise.

Lurking below the surface of the river was a *Deinosuchus*. It is twice as big as *Appalachiosaurus* and armed with a huge mouth full of teeth. *Appalachiosaurus* will be lucky to survive.

Deinosuchus

By the late Cretaceous Period, dinosaurs definitely ruled the Earth. They still had to be careful near water, though—that was where *Deinosuchus* lurked.

Deinosuchus was a giant crocodile-like creature, just as big as the biggest predatory dinosaurs. It probably ambushed animals that came close to the water's edge. *Deinosuchus* ate whatever it could catch—even huge tyrannosaurs such as *Albertosaurus* and *Appalachiosaurus*.

FACT FILE

Alive: 80–73 million years ago
Order and Family: Crocodilia/Alligatoroidea
Length: 32 ft. 9 in. (10 m)
Height: 4 ft. (1.2 m)
Weight: 5.5 tons (5 t)
Diet: carnivorous
Fossils found: fragments, including parts of skulls and skeletons
Location: central United States

SCALE

Senior killer
Deinosuchus lived a relatively long time: maybe 50 years or more. For the first 35 years at least, it would have kept on growing.

Rapid attack
Deinosuchus could launch a surprise attack in seconds. Once in its jaws, any prey would be unlikely to escape.

Appalachiosaurus

Like all tyrannosaurs, *Appalachiosaurus* probably hunted by ambushing its prey. If its sudden attack did not succeed, it may also have chased prey quickly for short distances.

Once it caught its victim, *Appalachiosaurus*'s main weapon was its large head and teeth. It would have attacked with deep, powerful bites that could quickly disable its prey.

SCALE

Ridged snout
Appalachiosaurus had the unusual feature of six low crest lines running across its snout.

FACT FILE

Alive: 77 million years ago
Order and Family: Saurischia/ Tyrannosauroidea
Length: 23+ ft. (7+ m)
Height: 8+ ft. (2.4+ m)
Weight: 1.1+ tons (1+ t)
Diet: carnivorous
Fossils found: part of the skeleton of a juvenile (pre-adult) specimen
Location: Alabama

How large?
The only *Appalachiosaurus* ever discovered was a youngster. No one is certain how big an adult would have been.

Battle in the Lake

Gorgosaurus vs. *Euoplocephalus*

Gorgosaurus must be hungry: it normally hunts unarmed hadrosaurs. *Euoplocephalus* is definitely *not* unarmed. In fact, one blow from its heavy tail club and *Gorgosaurus* could find itself unable to walk.

Even if *Gorgosaurus* gets close enough, it still has to somehow bite through *Euoplocephalus*'s bony armor.

Gorgosaurus

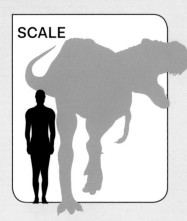

Fossils of young *Gorgosaurus* show that its shin bone was longer than its thigh bone. Other animals with this unusual adaptation are high-speed pursuit predators, so young *Gorgosaurus* may have hunted smaller, fast-moving prey.

By the time *Gorgosaurus* was fully grown, its thigh bone and shin bone were the same length. Its longer legs would still have allowed it to run fast, but now *Gorgosaurus* was hunting larger, slower prey—such as *Euoplocephalus*.

Horned brows
One of *Gorgosaurus*'s distinctive features was the little horned shapes above its eyes.

Fearsome bite
Gorgosaurus had about 60 large, sharp teeth, which helped it take deep bites of its prey.

KILLER FACT

Some *Gorgosaurus* walked with a limp. Fossils show they had broken a leg—which experts think may have been caused by hits from ankylosaurs such as *Euoplocephalus*.

FACT FILE

Alive: 77–75 million years ago
Order and Family: Saurischia/ Tyrannosauridae
Length: 26 ft. (8 m)
Height: 9 ft. 10 in. (3 m)
Weight: 2.75 tons (2.5 t)
Diet: carnivorous
Fossils found: skulls, parts of skeletons, and skin patches, so this dinosaur is completely known
Location: Alberta, Canada; Montana

Euoplocephalus

Watch out for that tail! Not only is it armed with a heavy club at the end, but the last half is stiffened by straight bones. If *Euoplocephalus* whacks you with it, a serious injury will be the result.

Its tail is not *Euoplocephalus*'s only defense against predators. Its head and body are also armored with osteoderms: thick, bony plates that are difficult to bite through.

SCALE

FACT FILE

Alive: 76–67 million years ago
Order: Ornithischia/Anklyosauridae
Length: 16 ft. (5 m)
Height: 5 ft. (1.5 m)
Weight: 2.2 tons (2 t)
Diet: herbivorous
Fossils found: complete skulls and skeletons
Location: Alberta, Canada; Montana

Shoulder spikes
The two large spikes above the dinosaur's shoulders prevented large predators from biting into its bony plates.

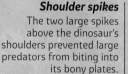

Wide mouth
Euoplocephalus's head was wider than it was long. Its very wide mouth was ideal for grabbing big mouthfuls of plants.

Believe It or Not!

Gorgosaurus may not have been a good parent

Experts think young *Gorgosaurus* avoided anywhere they might meet an adult—including their parents—for fear of being eaten! The youngsters seem to have lived for years hunting smaller prey without growing large. Then they grew to adult size very quickly.

Euoplocephalus was a dummy

No dinosaurs were smart, and most were probably less intelligent than animals such as wildebeest. Experts sometimes use a unit called EQ to measure likely intelligence. Humans have an EQ of 5.28. *Euoplocephalus*'s has been calculated at 0.52.

Tyrannosaurus had the WORST breath

Tyrannosaurus probably always had pieces of rotting meat trapped in its teeth. These would have smelled terrible—though if you were close enough to smell them, that wouldn't have been your biggest problem.

Plateosaurus leads the way

Plateosaurus was one of the first dinosaurs to be discovered (in 1834) and named (in 1837). It was also the first dinosaur ever discovered in Norway. The Norwegians must have been close to giving up on dinosaurs, until they found a Plateosaurus knucklebone in 2006.

Triceratops is worth a bundle!

Twenty years ago, if you wanted to buy a fossil *Triceratops* skull, it would have cost about $2,500 (£1,560). In 2007, the price had gone up to $25,000 (£12,500). And by 2015, a *Triceratops* skull was being offered for sale at a price of $1.8 million (£1.2 million)!

Appalachiosaurus was nearly called Albert

Well, *Albertosaurus*. When it was first discovered in 1982, experts thought it was a different North American tyrannosaur: the even bigger *Albertosaurus*. In 2005, though, it was decided that this was a new dinosaur, which was named *Appalachiosaurus* after the Appalachian region where it once roamed.

Survival mystery

Like dinosaurs and pterosaurs, crocodiles such as *Deinosuchus* were descended from the archosaurs—reptiles from the early Triassic Period. No one is sure why the crocodiles survived when the other branches of their family were wiped out 66 million years ago.

Dinosaur Descendants

The dinosaurs died out at the end of the Cretaceous Period . . . but did they die out completely? Or do creatures from the Age of Dinosaurs still stalk the Earth today?

Birds

Every time you see a bird fly by or peer at you from a tree, you're almost certainly looking into the eyes of a dinosaur descendant. Most experts now agree that today's birds probably have feathered dinosaurs somewhere in their family tree.

Anchiornis is the first known feathered dinosaur. Over time *Anchiornis* (or a dinosaur like it) probably began to use its feathers to help it climb trees in search of food, or to escape predators. Next came gliding down from trees, like *Microraptor*. Finally, the dinosaur descendant began to fly.

The most famous flyer from the time of the dinosaurs, *Archaeopteryx*, is sometimes called the first bird. But *Archaeopteryx* is very different from modern birds—other flyers that probably evolved from dinosaurs were much closer. *Confuciusornis*, for example, had the earliest beak we know about, plus stiff, rigid bones in its tail that supported feathers.

Sharks

The first sharks began to appear long before the end of the Cretaceous Period. In fact, their ancestors were swimming around before the dinosaurs even appeared. Then, about 200 million years ago, modern sharks began to spread throughout the oceans.

This means that today, if you meet a shark in an aquarium or out in the sea, you're eye to eye with a creature descended from the time when dinosaurs ruled the Earth.

Crocodiles and alligators

Today's crocodiles and alligators look very much like giant crocodilians (members of the crocodile family) from the age of the dinosaurs, such as *Sarcosuchus* or *Mourasuchus*—so are they descended from them?

Sadly for fans of the dinosaur era, the answer is no. The huge crocodilians died out alongside the dinosaurs they sometimes hunted. Today's crocs and alligators are descended from a very different branch of the crocodilian family tree.

Index

The Author

Paul Mason is a prolific author of children's books, many award-nominated, on such subjects as 101 ways to save the planet, vile things that go wrong with the human body, and the world's looniest inventors. Many contain surprising, unbelievable, or just plain revolting facts. Today, he lives at a secret location on the coast of Europe, where his writing shack usually smells of drying wetsuit (he's a former international swimmer and a keen surfer).

The Illustrator

Andre Leonard trained at Camberwell art school in London and at Leicester University. He has illustrated prolifically for leading magazines and book publishers, and his paintings are in a number of private collections worldwide. Andre prefers to work digitally but sometimes combines this with traditional media. He lives in Stamford, UK, with his wife, children, and a cat called Kimi, and he loves flying and sailing.

Glossary

apex predator: predator that no other animal naturally hunts

carnivorous: living on a diet of meat. Carnivorous dinosaurs probably all hunted for food, though some may also have eaten already-dead animals.

Crocodilia: group of reptiles that contains crocodiles, alligators, caimans and other similar animals

family: label given to groups of dinosaurs that had similar physical characteristics but were not exactly alike

fossil: remains of a living thing from long ago. Fossils can be the remains of bones, shells, pieces of wood, and plants—there are even fossilized footprints.

herbivorous: living on a diet of plants. Herbivorous dinosaurs would have been most plentiful wherever there was a good supply of plants and water.

neck frill: fan-shaped structure of skin and bone on the back of some dinosaurs' necks

order: one of two groups of dinosaurs, who were divided based on the way their hips worked

Ornithischia: one of the two orders of dinosaur. Ornithischian dinosaurs were "bird-hipped," with hips that looked similar to a bird's.

Saurischia: one of the two orders of dinosaur. Saurischian dinosaurs were "lizard-hipped," with hips that looked like a modern lizard's.

Picture credits